ON THE FIRST DAY
ONE LIGHT IS LIT
AND THEREAFTER THEY ARE
PROGRESSIVELY INCREASED.

BABYLONIAN TALMUD: SHABBAT 21b

THE LIGHTS OF HANUKKAH

BARBARA RUSH

A FAIR STREET BOOK

STEWART TABORI & CHANG

NEW YORK

Published in 2003 by
Stewart, Tabori & Chang
A Company of La Martinière Groupe
115 West 18th Street
New York, NY 10011

Export sales to all countries except Canada, France,
and French-speaking Switzerland:
Thames and Hudson Ltd.
181A High Holborn
London WC1V 7QX
England

Canadian Distribution:
Canadian Manda Group
One Atlantic Avenue, Suite 105
Toronto, Ontario M6K 3E7
Canada

Library of Congress Cataloging-in-Publication Data on file

ISBN: 1-58479-313-9

Produced by Fair Street Productions, New York City
Project Director, Editor: Susan Wechsler
Designer: Jon Glick
Photo Researcher: Sherri Zuckerman/Photosearch, Inc.
Copyeditor: Lesley Krauss

The text of this book was composed in Perpetua and Twentieth Century.

Printed in China

10 9 8 7 6 5 4 3 2 1

First Printing

PHOTO CREDITS
Art Resource, NY: 16, 20–21, 29, 32, 33, 34, 40, 48,
52, 62, 68, 79, 80–81, 87; (J. G. Berizzi) 18, 19, 22,
23, 35, 41, 45, 47, 54, 55, 56, 57, 61, 67; (Giraudon)
12; (Erich Lessing) 2, 9, 11, 14, 26, 28, 36–37, 43,
50–51, 53, 58–59, 69, 70-71, 75

Lelo Carter: 24-25, 72, 73, 78, 82–83, 85

Susan Einstein: 31, 60, 86, 88–89, 91

M. Lee Fatherree: 90

John Reed Forsman: 44, 49, 64–65

David Harris: 38–39, 76

Yoram Lehmann: 17

The Library of The Jewish Theological
Seminary of America: 6

CONTENTS

INTRODUCTION 7

THE GALLERY 15

EARLY 16

14TH CENTURY 18

16TH CENTURY 20

17TH CENTURY 24

18TH CENTURY 30

19TH CENTURY 48

20TH CENTURY 68

LIGHTING THE HANUKKAH MENORAH 92

BLESSINGS FOR HANUKKAH 93

READINGS AND SONGS FOR HANUKKAH 94

ACKNOWLEDGMENTS 96

INTRODUCTION

H A N U K K A H the joyous eight-day Jewish winter holiday (also called the Festival of Lights), begins on the 25th day of the Hebrew month Kislev. This festival, the second most widely celebrated of all Jewish home celebrations, is marked by special foods, games, songs, stories, and the giving of gifts. But the focus of the holiday is the religiously prescribed lighting of candles—on each of eight nights—in a special eight-branched candelabrum, commonly called a menorah (Hebrew for any lamp) or a Hanukkiah, the special Hanukkah lamp. Indeed, it is the Hanukkiah and its flickering lights that have kept Hanukkah alive for 2,000 years.

Quite probably the Hanukkah lights are remnants of a heathen winter solstice festival that, via torches and bonfires, brought much-needed light in the dark of winter. Hanukkah, as we know the Jewish festival, dates back to the second century B.C.E. and is the only historical festival not found in the Bible. It was documented instead in Book I and Book II of the Maccabees, written in the first century B.C.E. and first century C.E., respectively. These writings are part of the Apocrypha, a compilation of post-biblical semisacred books. In a weaving of history and legend, the story was interpreted and given new focus a few centuries later in the Babylonian Talmud, the second most sacred book after the Bible. Because of the complexity of various religious and political factors, students and scholars continue to debate the Hanukkah story today.

The story begins in 168 B.C.E., when the despot Antiochus IV (called Epiphanes, "The Risen God"), ruled the land later called Palestine. Antiochus was the Hellenized head of the Syrian branch of what had earlier been part of the large empire of Alexander the Great. Having decreed that all his subjects become Greek, Antiochus ordered that the Holy Temple in Jerusalem—site of Jewish religious life— be defiled with swine and that altars be built to Greek gods. Thus, he eliminated the Jewish practice of Torah, including circumcision and the Sabbath celebration.

In the town of Modi'in near Jerusalem, Mattathias, an elderly Jew and priest of the Hasmonean family, refused to perform the prescribed pagan rites. With a cry of "Let all who are for God follow me!" he, his five sons, and a band of followers fled to the hills and caves near Jerusalem. There for three years they fought boldly, and eventually, Mattathias' middle son, Judah, took command; his military prowess earned him the nickname "Maccabee," meaning hammer. On the 25th day of Kislev 165 B.C.E., the Maccabean force of only a few thousand defeated the mighty army of Antiochus; Jewish tradition had defeated Hellenism. By the light of a makeshift candelabrum, the victors cleansed the Temple, built altars for sacrifice, fashioned and lit a new seven-branched menorah, and rededicated the Temple (Hanukkah means "dedication") in an eight-day festival akin to Sukkot, distinguished by mirth, revelry, and prayers of thanksgiving to the Lord. Judah declared that a joyous eight-day celebration take place every year at this time. But thus far, there was no prescribed ritual for the celebration, no mention of kindling of lights on eight nights in an eight-branched lamp. So, where then, did this custom of lighting the Hanukkiah come from? The answer took several hundred years to develop.

Hasmonean rule continued for some generations but, about one hundred years after the Maccabean victory, Rome brought a new reign of terror upon the Jewish people. Decades of Jewish revolt had only increased Roman oppression—not only was the Second Temple destroyed in 70 C.E., but also many Jews were exiled to Babylonia and elsewhere. Additionally, later rebellions against Rome by those Jews left in Palestine failed, leaving the Jewish people in despair. An early part of the Talmud called the Mishnah (a compilation of the laws of the Torah) was written in Palestine, by permission of a relatively more benevolent Roman ruler. The Mishnah was completed by about 200 C.E. but, because mentioning a victory over foreign domination was politically unwise, the Mishnah contains almost no mention of Hanukkah. In third-century Babylonia, sages interpreting the few portions of the Mishnah that mention Hanukkah asked, "What is Hanukkah?" Their answers could no longer perpetuate a legend of ancient military victories and the dedication of a now-destroyed Temple. They sought instead a narrative with a spiritual message. These Talmudic sages drew upon earlier sources: the writings of Josephus, a Jewish historian of Roman times, who referred to the festival as "Lights," and the Scroll of Antiochus, a late-first-century rabbinic interpretation of the Hanukkah story that included an account about a jar of oil. And so, the Talmudists re-created the story of the oil and imbued it with the term "miracle":

And when the . . . Hasmonean kings vanquished (the Greeks), they searched and found no oil other than one small flask . . . . It contained just enough oil for one day. A miracle happened . . . , and they lit from it eight days. The next year they instituted these days as a holiday, with the reciting of the Hallel prayer and other thanks. (Babylonian Talmud: Shabbat 21b)

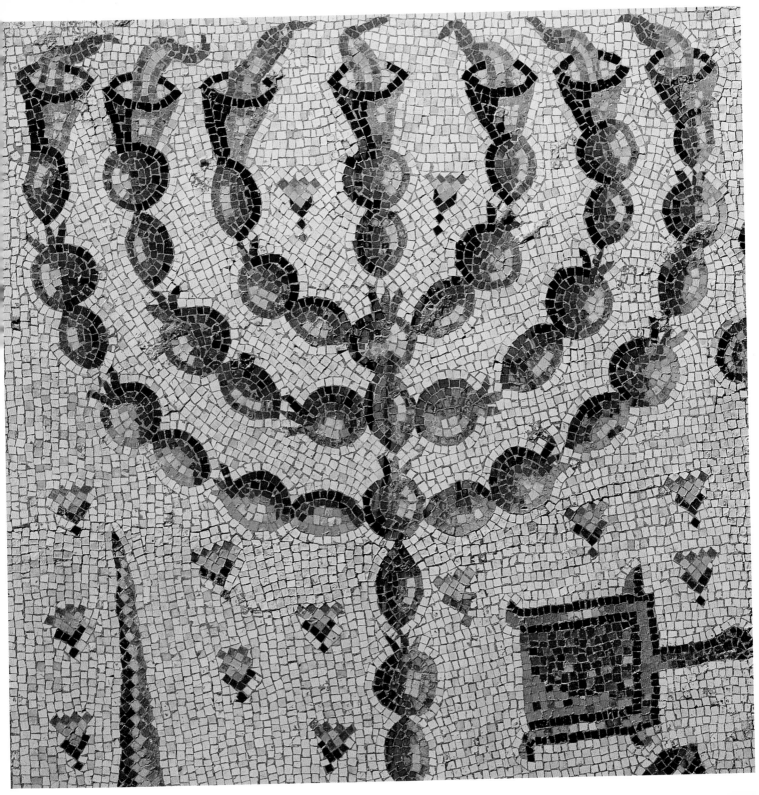

The message spread quickly: "Do not give up hope! A miracle can occur again!" Hanukkah, now a testament not to the Maccabees but to God, flourished in Palestine, in Babylonia, and in the rest of the Diaspora.

The Talmudists prescribed and fixed by law (mostly in the Tractate Shabbat of the Babylonian Talmud) the rules of how the holiday should be celebrated:

> The miracle of the oil must be proclaimed to the public.
>
> The sacred lights must be kindled in a specific order, first one light, ascending each night to eight.
>
> Lights must be separate from each other and in a row, so that no one night is more important than another.
>
> Lights should be kindled between "sunset and until no wayfarer is left in the street."
>
> Lights must burn for at least thirty minutes, and no reading, sewing, or other work is to be done by their illumination.

The prescriptions of the Talmud and later commentary changed the Hanukkah festival from a Temple celebration to one at home. They prescribed that Jews proclaim the miracle by displaying the Hanukkah lights in the street outside the door opposite the mezuzah (a religious amulet that protects the home). In times of danger (from non-Jewish neighbors) it is permissible to kindle the lights indoors and set them on a table. "Women are obligated to kindle since they took part in the miracle" (Shabbat 23a). In practice, in Sephardic[1] homes it became tradition for only the father (and sometimes other males) to kindle. Today, in many homes all over the world, everyone—young and old, male and female—lights candles, often in his or her own Hanukkah lamp.

All other customs of the festival—what to eat, stories to tell, songs to sing, games to play, etc.—are not prescribed by law but, rather, are embellishments by the folk—the people—over many centuries throughout the world.

SINCE THE TIME OF THE TALMUD the Hanukkah lamp has undergone many changes: for about one thousand years the lamp consisted of round or womb-shaped clay vessels with eight holes, or of a row of eight saucerlike receptacles. But during the Middle Ages the creative expression in making the Hanukkiah blossomed. During that period Hanukkah became an important and popular festival, possibly because of the message of hope it provided during times of harsh persecutions, the Crusades, and expulsions.

During the Middle Ages a ninth light was added to the eight already existing on the Hanukkah lamp. Since Talmudic injunction prohibits the kindling of one light with another, this new light—called the shammash[2] (servant in Hebrew)—acts as the attendant candle with which the other lights are lit. Also, because using the eight lights for illumination is forbidden, the light of the shammash may be used if one wants to read. To distinguish the shammash from the other candles, it is often placed higher on the lamp. Also, during the Middle Ages, the forms of the lamp continually evolved, from oil pots to a shape with a metal backplate for hanging, to a bench type that enabled the lamp to stand on its own.

The nine-branched candelabra-type Hanukkah lamp that emerged at this time was based upon the seven-branched gold menorah conventionally thought to have been one of the sacred vessels in the movable Tabernacle. This menorah was commanded by God to Moses, formed by Moses, and lit by Aaron during the wanderings of the Children of Israel through the wilderness. It is also thought to have been used both in the Temple of Solomon and, later, in the Second Temple, where it was kindled by the Maccabees in their festival of rededication. After the destruction of the Second Temple the menorah became an icon of Judaism. Its form is found on coins, synagogue floors, funerary art, and in graffiti of those ancient days. So too did it later beautify Sephardi and Ashkenazi manuscripts, serving as a

symbol of the Temple in Jerusalem to be rebuilt in days to come.

In modern times the menorah has become the symbol of the State of Israel, standing in gigantic form atop public buildings and imprinted on the coins, stamps, and medals of the State. Some people use the term "menorah" to describe not only the golden seven-branched lamp but also the nine-branched Hanukkah candelabrum; others use the term "Hanukkah menorah" or "Hanukkah lamp" or, as in Israel, "Hanukkiah," which, as the name suggests, is a lamp used for Hanukkah only.

For centuries after the Middle Ages, ornate Hanukkah lamps reflected Jewish wealth and the art and architecture of East and West. In the twentieth century, with the establishment of the State of Israel, Hanukkah became a national public holiday, creating a rise in the popularity of Hanukkah lamps. These were and still are being created with inventiveness and a modern flair.

Besides the prescription that on Hanukkah—no matter from which time or which culture—there be lights lit on eight nights, there is no other Talmudic requirement for the material, size, or decoration of the Hanukkiah. Expanding on the biblical passage: "This is my God and I will glorify Him" (Exodus 15:2), the Talmudists encouraged artistry and beauty in ceremonial objects. And, indeed, Hanukkiot, through the centuries, have been beautiful. Both folk and fine artists have creatively explored ways to present this lamp of eight lights, and the range over time of imagination in design and material has been extraordinary—from simple designs that mimic medieval architecture to ornate eighteenth-century rococo; from the most delicate and elaborate silver filigree to simple ceramic sculpture; from bullets of Israeli soldiers to the bottle caps and craft materials used by schoolchildren. Hanukkah lamps range in size from several inches to more than several feet; materials include gold, silver, and other precious metals, as well as wood, glass, and more; adornments, thought to protect the Hanukkiah and the idea of liberty, include strong animals, the seven-branched menorah, biblical quotes, scenes of the Maccabbean struggle, the crown of the Torah, and other Jewish symbols. These lamps represent the skills of and fine materials used by the most talented artists and craftspeople of each generation.

As a link to the past, the Hanukkah festival serves as a source of identification with Jews everywhere. Its meaning, whether secular, religious, or spiritual, has been interpreted in a myriad of ways. Some see it as a reminder of a military victory, especially of the few against the many; others identify it as a source of strength and assurance: Never again will Jews be overcome! It has stood as a sign of nationalism, a banner of religious freedom for all people, an affirmation of God's love of the people and their thanks for Divine intervention, and the messianic hope that new miracles will occur and that the Holy Temple will be rebuilt. The Hanukkah menorah represents God's Torah, of which light is always the symbol. And, finally, Hanukkah marks a time for a warm and happy embracing of family.

For all of these reasons Hanukkah remains timely today and timeless for the future. Modern Jews reiterate the holiday's personal message: How can I bring light out of darkness in my own life, and in the lives of others? How can I rededicate the world by making it a better place?

The Hanukkah festival, based on the Maccabean struggle, the combination of the miracle of a jar of oil, and the icon of the Temple, has had a resurgence in the United States in recent years. The most widely used Jewish celebratory object, the Hanukkiah—and the kindling of its lights—stands as the symbol of this happy holiday. The many different lamps shown in this book are joyous and creative expressions of this splendid celebration.

---

[1]Ashkenazim or Sephardim

In general, Ashkenazi(c) Jews, or Ashkenazim, are those Jews whose families came from Poland, Russia, Germany, and northern France. In general, Sephardi(c) Jews, or Sephardim, are those whose families came from Spain, and whose travels (after the expulsion in 1492) took them to countries such as Holland, southern France, North Africa, Greece, Italy, Turkey, and other countries. Some people use the term Sephardic to refer to all Jews who are not Ashkenazi.

[2]Shammash (sham mash´) is the modern Hebrew pronunciation as spoken in Israel. Jews whose families came from Eastern Europe may prefer to use the word shammes (sham´ mes), as pronounced in Yiddish and Eastern European Hebrew.

THE GALLERY

ALTHOUGH HANUKKAH LAMPS have been fashioned in different ways for centuries, most are decorated with symbols familiar to Jews all over the world. Many of the images that appear on the lamps bear witness to the destruction of the Holy Temple in 70 C.E., where the seven-branched menorah—later to become the foremost Jewish decorative art symbol—resided. Architectural structures—synagogues, churches, mosques, castles, palaces, and civic buildings—found on many menorahs symbolize the longing of the Jewish people to rebuild the ancient Temple.

Other decorations emphasize the reverence that Jewish people have for the Holy Book. The importance of Torah in Jewish life is often reinforced with imagery of biblical cherubim guarding the Ten Commandments, golden crowns glorifying the Torah, and the tree of life to which the Torah is likened. "For she (the Torah) is a tree of life," the prayer book tells us. The botanical motifs found on many lamps indicate ties to the Holy Land where, indeed, the Maccabean events took place. Trees such as oak, palm, and olive—the trees of Palestine—appear often. The biblical lion of Judah, a metaphor for God's strength, is another common adornment.

Since the Hanukkah menorah represents liberty and freedom—important principles in Jewish life that were fought for so boldly by the Maccabees—there is much iconography that symbolizes the enduring struggles and strength of the Jewish people.

16

ISRAEL, 4ᵀᴴ–5ᵀᴴ CENTURY

CLAY: MOLD-FORMED AND PULLED

Gift of the Betty and Max
Ratner Collection, 1981-75
The Jewish Museum, NY

Early oil lamps may have been used
for ceremonial purposes, but it is
uncertain whether any were used
to celebrate Hanukkah.

...Upon entering the Temple they found there eight
rods of iron which they grooved out and then kindled
wicks in the oil which they poured into the grooves.

(Midrash Pesikta Rabbati 2:13)

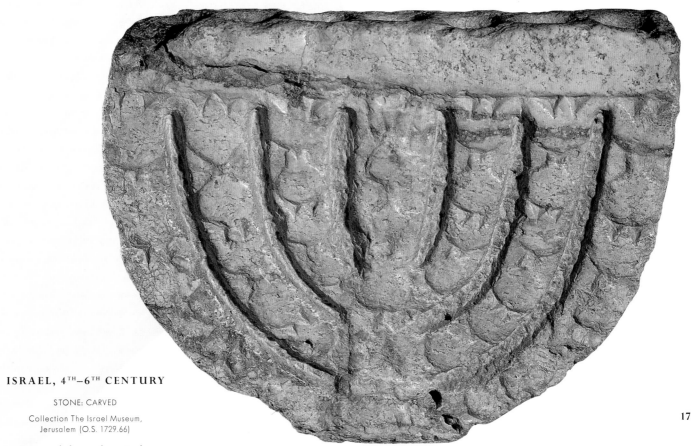

ISRAEL, 4ᵀᴴ–6ᵀᴴ CENTURY

STONE: CARVED

Collection The Israel Museum,
Jerusalem (O.S. 1729.66)

Some early lamps share similar
characteristics with Hanukkiot—for
instance, the lamp on the left contains
8 holes for oil. And although the lamp on
the right has only 7 oil holes, it
displays decorative motifs—bulbous
flowers and the seven-branched menorah
from the Temple of Solomon—found on
so many later Hanukkah lamps.

17

ITALY, 14TH CENTURY

BRONZE

Musée du Judaisme, Paris, France
Réunion des Musées Nationaux

Here the rampant lions protect the
flame that, according to a legend
known to the Jews of Italy,
represents the altar stolen from
the Holy Temple and hidden
by the Maccabees. The Hebrew
is from the Book of Proverbs (6:23).

**FRANCE OR SPAIN,
14ᵀᴴ CENTURY**

BRONZE

Musée du Judaisme, Paris, France
Réunion des Musées Nationaux

This early back-walled lamp is a blend
of two cultures. Although its basic
style is Spanish, the back wall and
windows reflect church architecture
of thirteenth-century France.

FOR THE COMMANDMENT
IS A LAMP AND THE
TEACHING IS A LIGHT.

(PROVERBS 6:23)

20   **ITALY, 16ᵀᴴ CENTURY**

BRASS: PIERCED

Gift of the Albert A. List Family
The Jewish Museum, NY

A lion sits upon the castle wall,
guarding the freedom that this lamp
represents. The Hebrew words are
from the book of Proverbs, quoted above.

ITALY, 16TH CENTURY

BRONZE

Musée du Judaisme, Paris, France
Réunion des Musées Nationaux

22

GERMANY, 16ᵀᴴ CENTURY   23

BRONZE

Musée du Judaisme, Paris, France
Réunion des Musées Nationaux

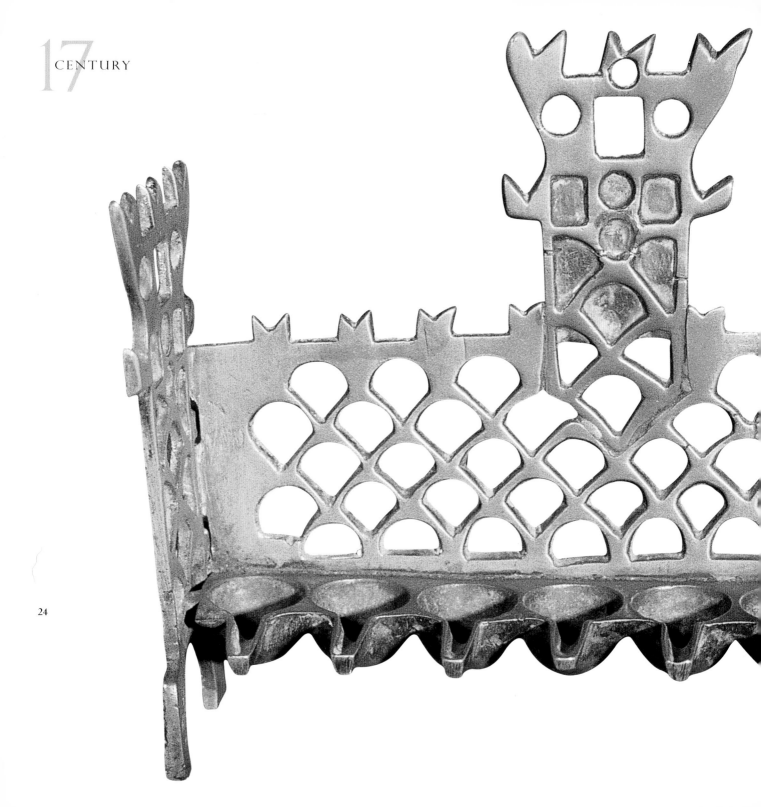

THE SANCTUARY WILL ON ANOTHER
OCCASION ALSO BE DEDICATED
BY THE LIGHTING OF CANDLES,
AND THEN IT WILL BE DONE BY THY
DESCENDANTS, THE HASMONEANS,
FOR WHOM I WILL PERFORM MIRACLES
AND TO WHOM I WILL GRANT GRACE....
THE LIGHTS OF THE HANUKKAH
FESTIVAL WILL SHINE FOREVER.

(MIDRASH, OR ZARUA 1:139)

ITALY, 17ᵀᴴ–18ᵀᴴ CENTURY

BRASS: CUTOUT

Gift of Dr. Lee M. Friedman
HUCSM 27.114
HUC Skirball Cultural Center,
Museum Collection, Los Angeles

25

These tall towers and crenellated
wall reflect the architecture of
early Renaissance Italy.

In medieval Venice, singers riding in
gondolas would stop by homes that
displayed a lit Hanukkiah and serenade
the occupants with Hanukkah songs.

AS THIS OIL BRINGS LIGHT TO THE WORLD,
SO DOES ISRAEL BRING LIGHT TO THE WORLD.

(MIDRASH CANTICLES RABBAH)

**EASTERN EUROPE,
17TH CENTURY**

SILVER: GILDED

Judaica Collection Max Berger, Vienna, Austria

The crowned lions of Judah
guard the Ten Commandments,
representing God's protection.

GERMANY, C.1680

JOHANN VALENTIN SCHULER

SILVER: GILDED

Gift of Norman S. Goetz, Henry A. Loeb,
Henry L. Marx, Ira A. Schur,
Lawrence A. Wien, Leonard Block,
Gustave L. Levy, Robert I. Wischnick
The Jewish Museum, NY

VENICE, ITALY, C.1650

BRONZE

Judaica Collection Max Berger, Vienna, Austria

This lamp portrays several scenes,
including Aaron lighting the
seven-branched menorah. The
central panel displays the Hebrew
prayer, "These lights we kindle,"
which Jews recite on Hanukkah
to remember God's miracle.

YOU ARE CLOTHED IN GLORY AND MAJESTY,

WRAPPED IN A ROBE OF LIGHT;...

(PSALMS 104:1, 2)

18TH CENTURY

BRONZE: CAST

Gift of Dr. Lee M. Friedman
HUCSM 27.122
HUC Skirball Cultural Center,
Museum Collection, Los Angeles

The Apocryphal book of Judith relates
the story of one woman's brave efforts
to save her people. Several centuries
before the Maccabean victory,
the Jews of Babylonia were surrounded
by enemies. Judith, a fair and lovely
widow, went to the enemy camp where
she made the chief captain, Holofernes,
drunk with wine, and then beheaded him.
Her depiction on Hanukkah lamps
commemorates her valor, inspiring the
idea that Hanukkah is a holiday for
women. In some Jewish communities,
women are given special gifts, and
are excused from work.

THE SYNAGOGUE IS A MICROCOSM, A REPLICA,
OF BOTH THE TABERNACLE AND THE TEMPLE.
AS GOD'S FIRST ACT WAS THE CREATION OF LIGHT,
SO "A SYNAGOGUE SHOULD HAVE A GREAT LIGHT."

(ZOHAR III:59b-60a)

**NORTH AFRICA,
18ᵀᴴ CENTURY**

BRASS: HAMMERED AND CUT

Gift of Dr. Harry G. Friedman
The Jewish Museum, NY

The hammered metal on the lamp is an
example of the excellent work of Jewish
metalsmiths in North Africa, and in
Morocco in particular. The Shield of
David, sometimes called the Jewish Star,
was a Jewish magical symbol in the Middle
Ages. Believed to have protective powers,
it was found on Kabbalistic amulets and on
many Hanukkah lamps in Morocco where
Kabbalah flourished. The star now appears
on the flag of the State of Israel, as an icon
of the Jewish people.

32

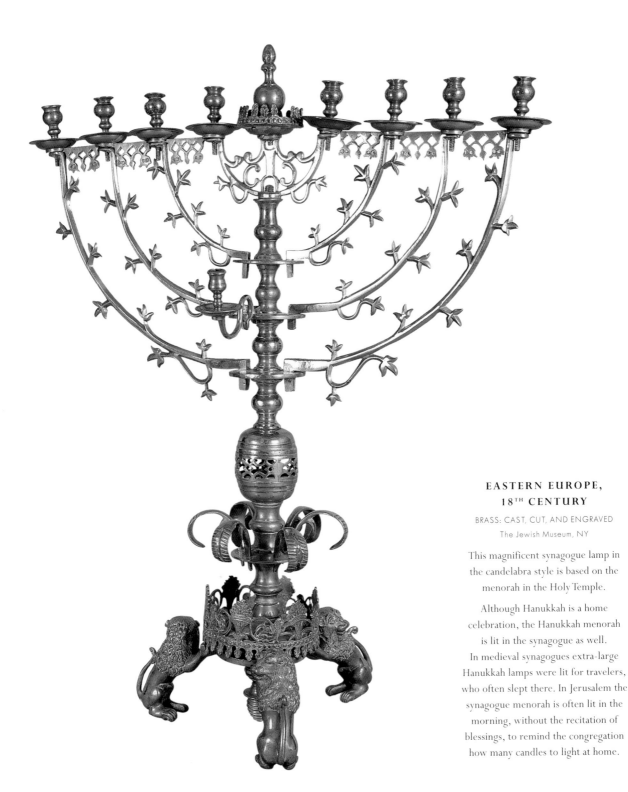

EASTERN EUROPE, 18TH CENTURY

BRASS: CAST, CUT, AND ENGRAVED
The Jewish Museum, NY

This magnificent synagogue lamp in the candelabra style is based on the menorah in the Holy Temple.

Although Hanukkah is a home celebration, the Hanukkah menorah is lit in the synagogue as well. In medieval synagogues extra-large Hanukkah lamps were lit for travelers, who often slept there. In Jerusalem the synagogue menorah is often lit in the morning, without the recitation of blessings, to remind the congregation how many candles to light at home.

33

HOLLAND, 18ᵀᴴ CENTURY

BRASS

Victoria and Albert Museum, London

The ornate work on this lamp typifies the scrolls, floral decorations, and shells of the rococo style. It has a bucket to hold the drippings from the burning oil.

In Europe, the melted wax from candles used on Yom Kippur, the holiest day of the Jewish year, was sometimes reused to create candles for Hanukkah.

ITALY, 18ᵀᴴ CENTURY

BRONZE

Musée du Judaisme, Paris, France
Réunion des Musée Nationaux

ARISE, SHINE,
FOR YOUR LIGHT HAS DAWNED,
THE PRESENCE OF THE LORD
HAS SHONE UPON YOU!

(ISAIAH 60:1)

UKRAINE, 18TH CENTURY

SILVER: FILIGREED AND PARTLY GILDED

Judaica Collection Max Berger, Vienna, Austria

The double shammash on this
lamp is typical of the Hanukkah
lamps of the Ukraine. But the double
shammash also appears on menorahs
from other cultures. In Aleppo, Syria,
an extra shammash was added to the
Hanukkah menorah to thank and praise
God for protecting those who fled
Spain during the expulsion. Gratitude
was also expressed for bringing those
Jews safely to Syria.

37

IRAQ, 18ᵀᴴ CENTURY

BRASS: CAST WITH RINGS FOR
GLASS OIL HOLDERS (NOT PICTURED)

Gift of Dr. A. Ticho Collection, Jerusalem
The Israel Museum, Jerusalem

A type of Hanukkiah with five hands
(or *hamsa*) developed in North Africa,
Iraq, and Syria. The word "*hamsa*" is related
to the Hebrew and Arabic word "five."
In Hebrew the fifth letter of the alphabet,
hay (ה), is one of the visual ways of
representing the name of God; this letter
also appears two times in another name of
God, יהוה. The *hamsa* is considered
good luck, as it brings God's protection
and wards off the evil eye. In Syria,
candles shaped like the *hamsa* are lit in addition to the lights of the Hanukkiah.

GERMANY, 18ᵀᴴ CENTURY

JOHANN ADAM BOLLER

SILVER: CAST, ENGRAVED, FILIGREED,
HAMMERED, AND GILDED,
WITH ENAMEL PLAQUES

Gift of Mrs. Felix Warburg
The Jewish Museum, NY

The enamel plaques at the base
depict the bravery of Jacob.

GERMANY, 18ᵀᴴ CENTURY

JOHANN MICHAEL SCHÜLER

SILVER: EMBOSSED

Musée du Judaisme, Paris, France
Réunion des Musées Nationaux

Judith, holding the head of Holofernes,
sits atop these magnificent lamps.
The bulbous forms and flowers
echo the decorations of the
Tabernacle's menorah as described
in the book of Exodus.

THEY CELEBRATED IT FOR EIGHT DAYS WITH REJOICING
IN THE MANNER OF THE FEAST OF TABERNACLES...

(II MACCABEES 10: 6)

42   **GERMANY, 18TH CENTURY**

SILVER

Judaica Collection Max Berger,
Vienna, Austria

Powerful mythological animals—such as
this eight-headed peacock—often appear
on Hanukkah lamps to offer protection.

POLAND, 18ᵀᴴ CENTURY

SILVER: REPOUSSÉ

Museum Purchase
HUCSM 27.100
HUC Skirball Cultural Center,
Museum Collection, Los Angeles

This exquisite lamp displays fine
metalsmithing from Eastern Europe,
where Jews were permitted to learn
such skills. In addition to their
religious studies, Jews were also allowed
to study the natural sciences. This tree
of life is a realistic depiction of
the animals and plants of the forest.

FRANCE, 18ᵀᴴ CENTURY

COPPER

Musée du Judaisme, Paris, France
Réunion des Musées Nationaux

45

ONE WHO LIGHTS THE HANUKKAH CANDLE
MUST RECITE A BLESSING...
ONE WHO SEES THE HANUKKAH CANDLE
MUST [ALSO] RECITE A BLESSING.

(BABYLONIAN TALMUD: SHABBAT 23a)

HOLLAND, 18TH CENTURY

COPPER: REPOUSÉE

Musée du Judaisme, Paris, France
Réunion des Musées Nationaux

Hanukkah lamps from Holland and
North Africa are similar because Jews
expelled from Spain fled to both places,
bringing with them the influence of
Moorish art. The open metal work
on this Hanukkiah is one example.
The first blessing for kindling the lights
appears along with the lions and crown.

ברוך אתה ה'
אלהינו מלך העולם
אשר קדשנו במצותיו וצונו
להדליק נר של חנוכה

GERMANY, 1814

HIRSCH HANUKKAH LAMP

SILVER: REPOUSSÉ, PIERCED, AND CAST

Museum Purchase
HUCSM 27.70
HUC Skirball Cultural Center,
Museum Collection, Los Angeles

This lamp, a miniature building,
reflects the architecture prevalent
in early nineteenth-century Europe.
The three Hanukkah blessings are
written at the bottom of the menorah.

48

AUSTRIA,
18ᵀᴴ–19ᵀᴴ CENTURY

JOSEF KOHN

SILVER: REPOUSSÉ, CHASED, AND CAST

Gift of Harry G. Friedman.
The Jewish Museum, NY

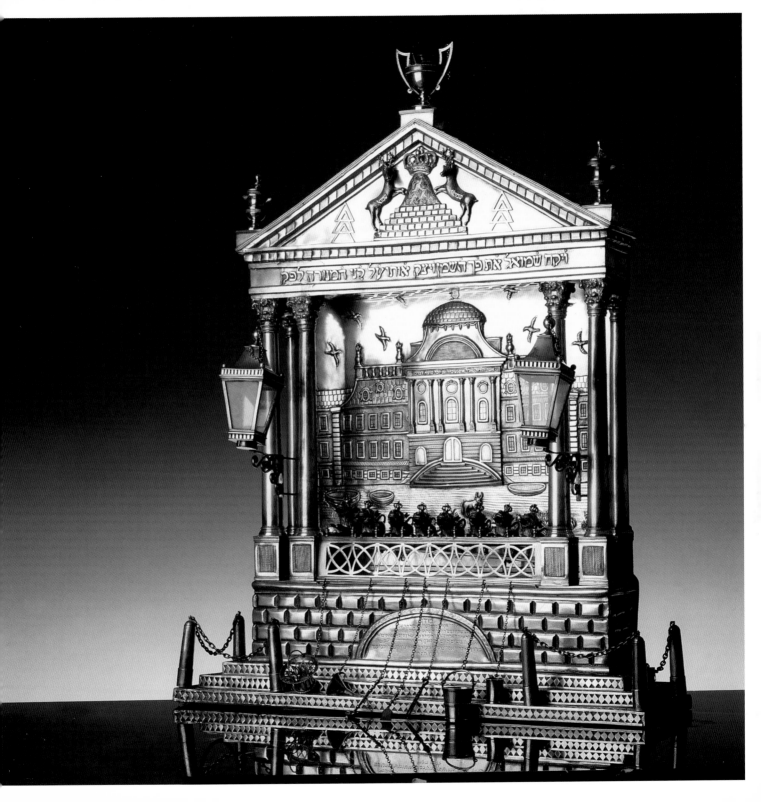

THE CANDLES AND OIL ARE
NOT INTRINSICALLY HOLY.
IT IS ONLY THROUGH
THEIR USE THAT THEY
BECOME HOLY.

RABBI MEIR OF ROTHENBURG

50

AUSTRIA, 19ᵀᴴ CENTURY

SILVER

Judaica Collection Max Berger, Vienna, Austria

CZECH REPUBLIC, 1817

SILVER

Judaica Collection Max Berger,
Vienna, Austria

**EASTERN EUROPE,
19TH CENTURY**

BRONZE: CAST

The Rose and Benjamin Mintz Collection
The Jewish Museum, NY

This lamp presents Paradise—the
palm trees of the Land of Israel and a
zoological garden of strong animals,
including deer, elephants, lions, griffins,
gorillas, and bears. The open metalwork
reflects paper cutting, a popular
craft among Jews in Eastern Europe.

52   WHEN ALL THE CANDLES ARE BURNING BRIGHT,
ONE MUST MARVEL AND REJOICE AT THE ACCOMPLISHED WORK.
AND NO TASK MAKES ONE HAPPIER THAN BEING A SERVANT OF LIGHT

(THEODOR HERZL, "THE MENORAH")

AUSTRIA-HUNGARY, 1818

SILVER: PARTIALLY GILDED

Musée du Judaisme, Paris, France
Réunion des Musées Nationaux

In the center panel appear
the words of the prayer, "We kindle
these lights to remind us of the
miracles"... God wrought in
the days of the Maccabees.

**CENTRAL EUROPE
EARLY 19ᵀᴴ CENTURY**

SILVER

Musée du Judaisme, Paris, France
Réunion des Musées Nationaux

**MOROCCO,
19TH CENTURY**

BRONZE

Musée des Arts d'Afrique
et d'Oceanie, Paris, France
Réunion des Musées Nationaux

This engraved lamp, representative
of Moroccan jewelry, also features
designs that mirror the embroidery
found on bags for carrying prayer shawls.

UKRAINE, 19ᵀᴴ CENTURY

SILVER

Musée du Judaisme, Paris, France
Reunion des Musées Nationaux

The crown, an important symbol
in Jewish art, is associated
with the power of God.

YOUR WORD IS A LAMP
TO MY FEET.

(PSALMS 119:105)

58   **HOLLAND, c. 1840**

SILVER

Judaica Collection Max Berger
Vienna, Austria

POLAND, 19ᵀᴴ CENTURY

BRASS: CAST AND TURNED
HUCSM 27.62
HUC Skirball Cultural Center,
Museum Collection, Los Angeles

Thirty-six candles (not counting the
shammash) are kindled during the
Hanukkah festival. Some think that a
connection exists between the number
of sacred candles and the thirty-six just
souls whose goodness—according to
Jewish tradition—keeps the world going.

61

CENTRAL EUROPE, C. 1863

SILVER: FILIGREED AND PARTIALLY GILDED

Musée du Judaïsme, Paris, France,
Réunion des Musées Nationaux

Proud lions form the oil holders on
this delicate and graceful lamp.

WE SEE THAT A CANDLE, A WICK, AND OIL GIVE FORTH
LIGHT THROUGH DIMINISHING. LIKEWISE, THE MAN
WHO LIMITS HIS MATERIAL WANTS TO MINIMUM,
MAY GIVE OUT SPIRITUAL LIGHT.

(THE GERER RABBI)

AUSTRIA, 1872–1892

HG, FIRM OF BETTY BETTELHEIM

SILVER: CUTOUT, REPOUSSÉ,
ENGRAVED, AND CHASED

Gift of Mrs. Rosemarie Melchior
in memory of her father,
Eugene Joseph Margolin
The Jewish Museum, NY

THE SPIRIT OF MAN IS THE LAMP OF THE LORD.

(PROVERBS 20:27)

**GERMANY
19ᵀᴴ–20ᵀᴴ CENTURY**

PEWTER AND BRASS: CAST

Kirschstein Collection
HUCSM 27.47
HUC Skirball Cultural Center,
Museum Collection, Los Angeles

These individual chair-shaped oil
lamps bear the inscription,
Ner Hanukkah, a light of Hanukkah.
Hanukkah lamps made of individual
receptacles are rooted in the lamps
of ancient times. Until recently
Jews from the areas of Persia and
Afghanistan did not use a one-piece
Hanukkiah; instead, they used
eight saucers set in a row, each
with a wick and filled with oil.

64

MOROCCO,
19TH–20TH CENTURY

BRASS: ENGRAVED

Musée du Judaisme, Paris, France
Réunion des Musées Nationaux

Design features such as Moorish arches
and prayer niches typify Spanish
decorative art, and can be seen on the
Hanukkah lamps of North Africa, Holland,
France, the Middle East, and even on
those from India and the New World.
Jews traveled to all these places after
their expulsion from Spain in 1492.

68 **UNITED STATES, C.1900**

TIN: CAST AND BRASS-PLATED

Gift of Harry G. Friedman
The Jewish Museum, NY

The American eagle, an icon of
American liberty, is linked to the freedom
celebrated in the Hanukkah story.

AND NATIONS SHALL
WALK BY YOUR LIGHT,
KINGS, BY YOUR
SHINING RADIANCE.

(ISAIAH 60:3)

HUNGARY, C.1900

SILVER

Judaica Collection Max Berger, Vienna, Austria

70

On this exquisite jeweled lamp,
the shammash is in the form of a
genie's lamp, capable of granting
the owner's wishes and dreams.

Any pure oil can be used to kindle
the Hanukkah lamp, but olive oil
(as found in Palestine and used
by the Maccabees to light the
Temple menorah) is preferred.

ISRAEL, C.1900

BRASS AND GLASS

Gift of Audrey Skirball-Kenis
HUCSM 27.208 a-j
HUC Skirball Cultural Center,
Museum Collection, Los Angeles

This lamp is reminiscent of the
Hanukkah lamps from Talmudic times,
when lights were enclosed in a lantern
for protection from the wind.

GERMANY,
C.1900

SILVER: DIE-STAMPED, ENGRAVED,
AND SHEET IRON

Gift of the Jewish Cultural
Reconstruction, Inc.
HUCSM 27.95
HUC Skirball Cultural Center,
Museum Collection, Los Angeles

The shape of the traditional Triumphal
Arch is a fitting reference to the
triumphant victory of
the Maccabean army.

HOW PLEASANT ARE YOU WITH THE HANUKKAH LAMP.

(BABYLONIAN TALMUD: SOFERIM 20:3)

20TH CENTURY

CERAMIC: GLAZED

Judaica Collection Max Berger
Vienna, Austria

WITH YOU IS THE FOUNTAIN OF LIFE;
BY YOUR LIGHT DO WE SEE LIGHT.

(PSALMS 36:10)

ALGERIA, 1932

LALOUK KALIF

COPPER AND BRASS:
PIERCED AND ENGRAVED

Gift of Zeyde Schulmann Collection, Paris, 1963
Collection Israel Museum, Jerusalem

This stunning architectural lamp
exemplifies the skills of Jewish metal
artisans living in North Africa,
where the moon and crescent
symbolize the Islamic world.

77

GERMANY, 1945-1947

CERAMIC: GLAZED

Jewish Joint Distribution Committee
Gift in Memory of Jean Segal Caplan
HUCSM 27.167
HUC Skirball Cultural Center,
Museum Collection, Los Angeles

On this beautiful lamp, a tree trunk, split
in two, states the political situation in
post–World War II Germany, when the
country was divided into East and West.
As every Hanukkah lamp is the symbol of
freedom, so too does this lamp stand as
hope for freedom in a united Germany.

ISRAEL, C.1930

BEZALEL SCHOOL

BRASS: HAMMERED,
EMBOSSED, AND PUNCHED

Gift of Harry G. Friedman
The Jewish Museum, NY

Bezalel, a skilled craftsman in
biblical times, fashioned the
wandering Tabernacle carried
through the wilderness by the
children of Israel. (Exodus 35: 30–35)
Jerusalem's fine academy of art
now bears his name.

78

UNITED STATES, 1974

MAE SHAFTER ROCKLAND

WOOD: FABRIC-COVERED WITH
MOLDED PLASTIC FIGURES

Gift of the artist, 1984
Coxe and Go/The Jewish Museum, NY

The Statue of Liberty on this lamp
symbolizes both American liberty,
valiantly fought for, and liberty sought
and won by the Jews in Maccabean times.

80

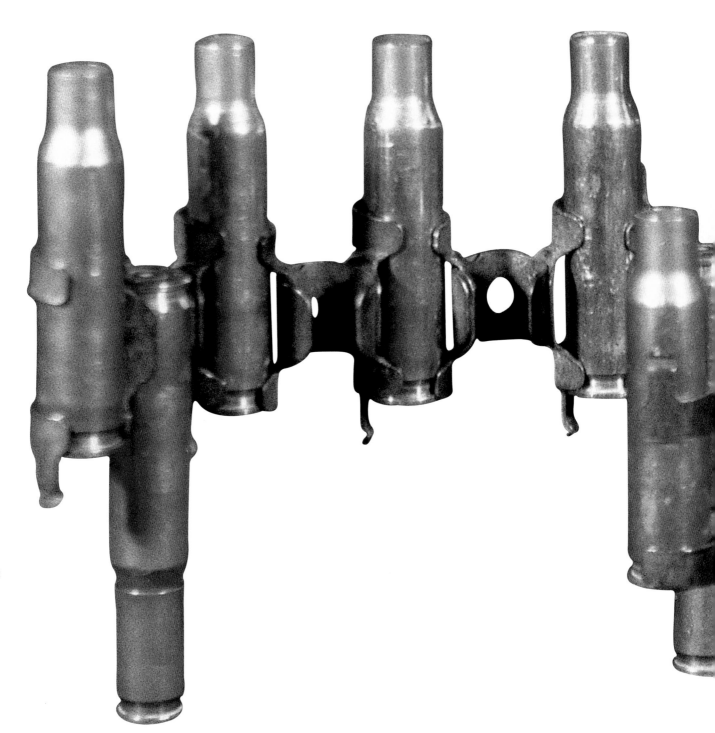

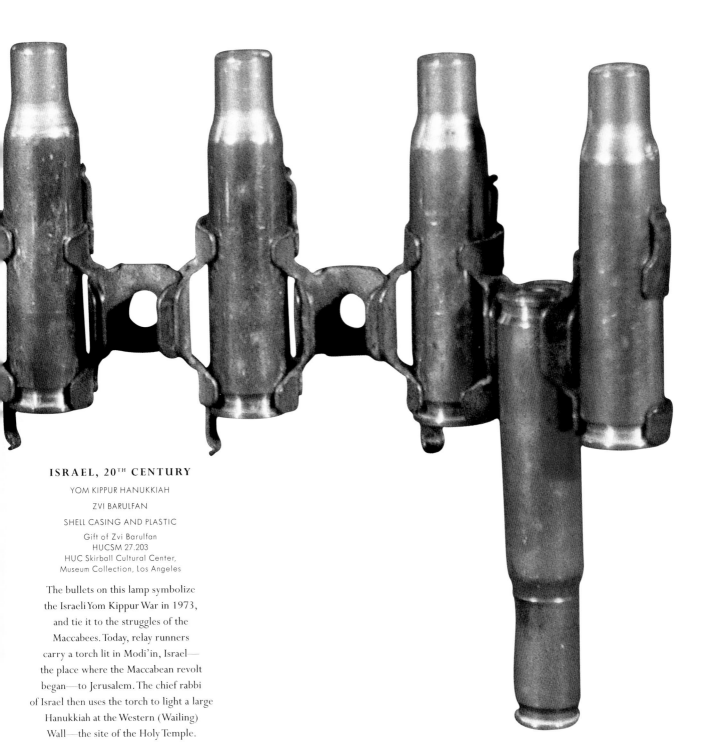

ISRAEL, 20ᵀᴴ CENTURY

YOM KIPPUR HANUKKIAH

ZVI BARULFAN

SHELL CASING AND PLASTIC

Gift of Zvi Barulfan
HUCSM 27.203
HUC Skirball Cultural Center,
Museum Collection, Los Angeles

The bullets on this lamp symbolize
the Israeli Yom Kippur War in 1973,
and tie it to the struggles of the
Maccabees. Today, relay runners
carry a torch lit in Modi'in, Israel—
the place where the Maccabean revolt
began—to Jerusalem. The chief rabbi
of Israel then uses the torch to light a large
Hanukkiah at the Western (Wailing)
Wall—the site of the Holy Temple.

83

PROCLAIM LIBERTY THROUGHOUT THE LAND
AND UNTO ALL THE INHABITANTS THEREOF.

(LEVITICUS 25:10)

UNITED STATES, 1990s

LIBERTY BELL HANUKKAH LAMP

MANFRED ANSON

84   BRONZE

Museum Purchase with funds provided
by the Peachy and Mark Levy Project
Americana Acquisition Fund
HUCSM 27.193
HUC Skirball Cultural Center,
Museum Collection, Los Angeles

In this contemporary American
lamp, Liberty bells symbolize the
freedom of the Maccabees, the
Americans, and the Jewish people.

85

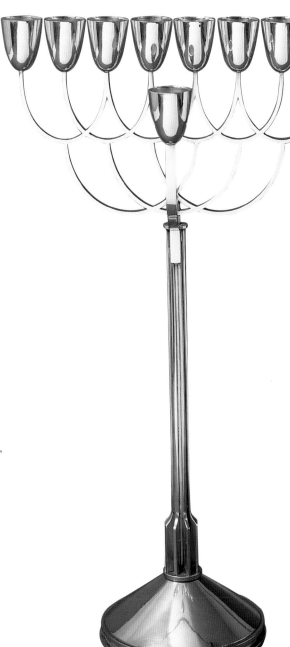

**UNITED STATES,
20ᵀᴴ CENTURY**

LUDWIG WOLPERT

SILVER

Museum purchase with funds
provided by the Wilma and
Howard Friedman Acquisition fund,
in memory of Jeanette Sanditen Mann
HUCSM 27.131
HUC Skirball Cultural Center,
Museum Collection, Los Angeles
Courtesy of Chava Wolpert Richard

These modern lamps, by a
renowned twentieth-century artisan,
are an interpretation of the
candelabra-style Hanukkiah.

**UNITED STATES,
C.1957**

LUDWIG WOLPERT

SILVER

Collection of the Newark Museum,
Gift of the Friends of the Robison Institute
of The Newark YMHA and
of The Newark Museum, 1957
The Newark Museum, NJ
Courtesy of Chava Wolpert Richard

THEREFORE, HONOR THE LORD WITH LIGHT.

(ISAIAH 24:15)

UNITED STATES, 1990

RICHARD MEIER

TIN

Museum purchase with funds provided by Audrey
and Arthur N. Greenberg Acquisition Fund
HUCSM 27.168
HUC Skirball Cultural Center,
Museum Collection, Los Angeles

89

Designed by a well-known American
architect, this sculptural Hanukkiah
contains a series of reductive
architectural forms; each one
represents a time and place in Jewish
history—from antiquity to the present.

A MIRACLE OCCURRED AND THE SUPPLY LASTED EIGHT DAYS.

(BABYLONIAN TALMUD: SHABBAT 21b)

UNITED STATES, 1995

MENORAH, 1995

MARVIN LIPOFSKY

GLASS

Gift of Andrea and Charles Bronfman
HUCSM 27.198 a-c
HUC Skirball Cultural Center,
Museum Collection, Los Angeles

These abstract sculptural forms by a well-known glass artist create an imaginative Hanukkah setting for the burning candles.

UNITED STATES, 20TH CENTURY

PETER SHIRE

STEEL, ENAMEL, AND ANODIZED ALUMINUM

Gift of the Comess and
Comess-Daniels Families
HUCSM 27.192
HUC Skirball Cultural Center,
Museum Collection, Los Angeles

This playful modern lamp features the dove of peace sent forth by Noah to find dry land (Genesis 8:8-11). The dove is also a symbol of the Divine Presence that brought deliverance to the Jewish people in the Hanukkah story.

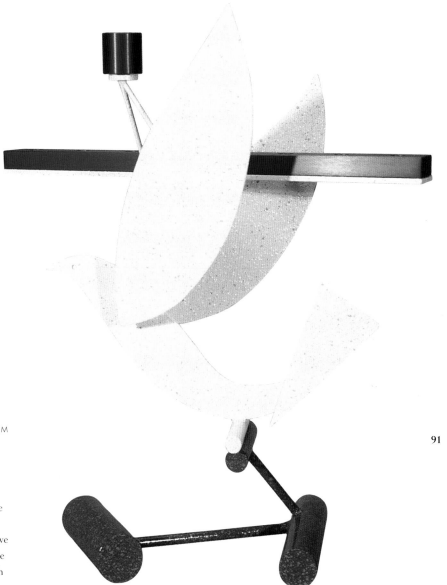

91

LIGHTING THE HANUKKAH MENORAH

Pronunciation

H in the word *Hanukkah* has the guttural *ch* sound in Hebrew.

Ch, as in the word *Baruch*, has a similar guttural sound.

DIRECTIONS FOR KINDLING THE LIGHTS:

On the first night:

- Face the menorah.
- Place a candle in the place for the shammash.
- Place a candle on the far right.
- Light the shammash.
- Recite all three blessings.
- Using the shammash, light the one candle on the right.
- Replace the shammash.

On all other nights:

- Face the menorah.
- Place a candle in the place for the shammash.
- Place two candles on the far right. (Three on the third night, etc.)
- Light the shammash.
- Recite the first two blessings.
- Using the shammash, light the candles from *left to right*.
- Replace the shammash.

BLESSINGS FOR HANUKKAH

Baruch atah Adonai elohaynu melech ha'olam asher kid'shanu
b'mitzvotav v'tzivanu l'hadlik ner shel Hanukkah.

Praised are You, Adonai our God, Sovereign of the Universe, who has made us holy by
mitzvot and instructed us to kindle the lights of Hanukkah.

בָּרוּךְ אַתָּה יהוה אֱלֹהֵינוּ מֶלֶךְ הָעוֹלָם,

אֲשֶׁר קִדְּשָׁנוּ בְּמִצְוֹתָיו וְצִוָּנוּ לְהַדְלִיק נֵר שֶׁל חֲנֻכָּה.

Baruch atah Adonai elohaynu melech ha'olam she'asah nisim
lavotaynu bayamim hahaym bazman hazeh.

Praised are You, Adonai our God, Sovereign of the Universe, who performed miracles
for our ancestors in days of old, at this time of year.

בָּרוּךְ אַתָּה יהוה אֱלֹהֵינוּ מֶלֶךְ הָעוֹלָם, שֶׁעָשָׂה נִסִּים

לַאֲבוֹתֵינוּ בַּיָּמִים הָהֵם בַּזְּמַן הַזֶּה.

On the first night only, add:

Baruch atah Adonai elohaynu melech ha'olam sheh-heh-cheh-yanu
v'ki'y'manu v'higiyanu lazman hazeh.

Praised are You, Adonai our God, Sovereign of the Universe, who has kept us alive,
sustained us, and enabled us to reach this day.

בָּרוּךְ אַתָּה יהוה אֱלֹהֵינוּ מֶלֶךְ הָעוֹלָם,

שֶׁהֶחֱיָנוּ וְקִיְּמָנוּ וְהִגִּיעָנוּ לַזְּמַן הַזֶּה.

READINGS AND SONGS FOR HANUKKAH

Traditionally, the blessings are followed by the recitation or singing of Hanerot Hallalu, *based on a text from the* Talmud.

HANEROT HALLALU (These Lights . . .)

We kindle these lights to remain mindful of the miracles, and the wonders, and the battles You helped win for our ancestors in their days, at this season. During all eight days of Hanukkah these lights are sacred, and we may not make any use of them, except to look upon them, in order to thank You and praise Your name for Your miracles and for Your wonders, and for Your deliverance.

Traditionally, after Hanerot Hallalu, *Ashkenazim sing, "Rock of Ages," a thirteenth-century German hymn. Some Sephardim also include this song in their celebration.*

ROCK OF AGES

Rock of Ages, let our song

Praise your saving power;

You, amid the raging foe,

Were our shelt'ring tower.

Furious they assailed us,

But your arm availed us,

And your word

Broke their sword

When our own strength failed us.

It is customary for Sephardim to recite Psalm 30, written by King David, and thought to have been recited when Solomon, his son, dedicated the First Temple. It is also said to have been recited by the Maccabees upon their rededication of the Temple.

PSALM 30

I extol You, O Lord,

for You have lifted me up,

and not let my enemies rejoice over me.

O Lord, my God,

I cried out to You,

and You healed me.

O Lord, You brought me up from Sheol,

preserved me from going down into the Pit. . . .

You turned my lament into dancing,

You undid my sackcloth and girded me with joy,

that (my) whole being might sing hymns to You endlessly;

O Lord my God, I will praise You forever.

To my grandchildren: Seth, Cheryl, Ishayah, Shoshi, Ilan, Cobi, and Hana.
May their continued Hanukkah celebrations be filled with light and joy.

ACKNOWLEDGMENTS

Special thanks to my husband, Don, for acting as a sounding board and a source of encouragement, and for volunteering his computer know-how and research skills, without which this book would not have come to be.

To the following people who made this book possible I am most grateful: Rabbi Zalman Bluming and Yehudis Bluming, Sarah Font, Dov and Haya Gavish, Jon Glick (designer), Fred and Ingrid Hertz, Atarah Jablonsky, Anne Kostick (Stewart, Tabori & Chang), Rina and Azariah Levy, Cherie Karo Schwartz, Howard Schwartz, Hannah Shatz, Simcha Shemesh, Sue Speier, Susan Wechsler (Fair Street Productions), Sheva Zucker, Sherri Zuckerman (Photosearch, Inc.).

And thanks to the museums and collections from which these beautiful art works were selected, and, in particular, to Susanne Kester and Grace Cohen-Grossman from the Skirball Museum, Ziva Haller from the Israel Museum, and Gerhard Guitrooy from Art Resource for their special efforts on our behalf.

The author acknowledges the following writers and editors whose works were essential to the research project: I.A. Agus, Nathan Ausubel, Nancy M. Berman, Abraham P. Bloch, Theodor H. Gaster, Louis Ginsberg, Philip Goodman, Freema Gottlieb, Norman L. Kleeblatt, Vivian Mann, Louis I. Newman, Lesli Koppelman Ross, Hayyim Schauss, Arthur Waskow, and David Zaslow.

Sources consulted include prayer books of the Conservative, Jewish Renewal, Orthodox, Reconstructionist, and Reform movements. Bible excerpts reprinted from the *Tanakh: The Holy Scriptures, The New Translation According to the Traditional Hebrew Text*, ©1999, by the Jewish Publication Society.

THEY DECREED BY EDICT AND CONFIRMED BY VOTE THAT THE ENTIRE NATION OF THE JEWS SHOULD CELEBRATE THESE DAYS EVERY YEAR.

(II MACCABEES 10:8)